AF577266
5

HINTS

As in all crocheted pieces, good finishing techniques make a big difference in the quality of the piece. Make a habit of taking care of loose ends as you work. Thread a tapestry needle with the thread end. With **wrong** side facing, weave the needle through several stitches, then reverse the direction and weave it back through several stitches. When ends are secure, clip them off close to work.

JOINING WITH SC

When instructed to join with sc, begin with a slip knot on hook. Insert hook in stitch or space indicated, YO and pull up a loop, YO and draw through both loops on hook.

JOINING WITH DC

When instructed to join with dc, begin with a slip knot on hook. YO, holding loop on hook, insert hook in stitch or space indicated, YO and pull up a loop (3 loops on hook), (YO and draw through 2 loops on hook) twice.

BACK LOOP ONLY

Work only in loop(s) indicated by arrow ***(Fig. 1)***.

Fig. 1

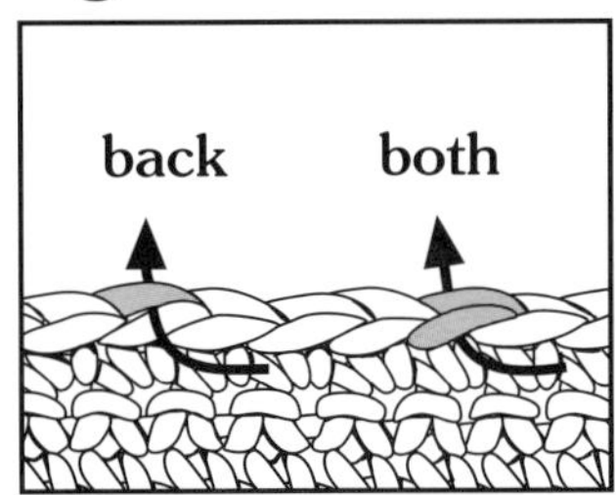

BACK RIDGE

Work only in loops indicated by arrows ***(Fig. 2)***.

Fig. 2

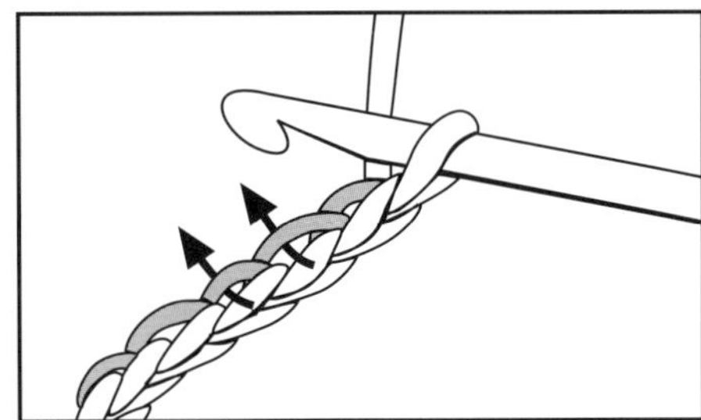

FREE LOOPS OF A CHAIN

When instructed to work in free loops of a chain, work in loop indicated by arrow ***(Fig. 3)***.

Fig. 3

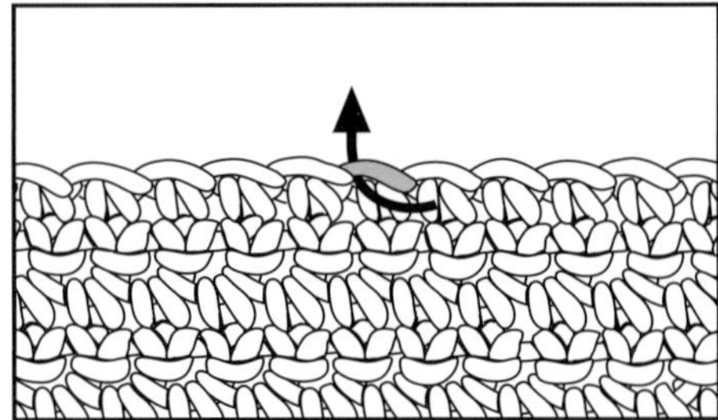

POST STITCH

Work around post of stitch indicated, inserting hook in direction of arrow ***(Fig. 4)***.

Fig. 4

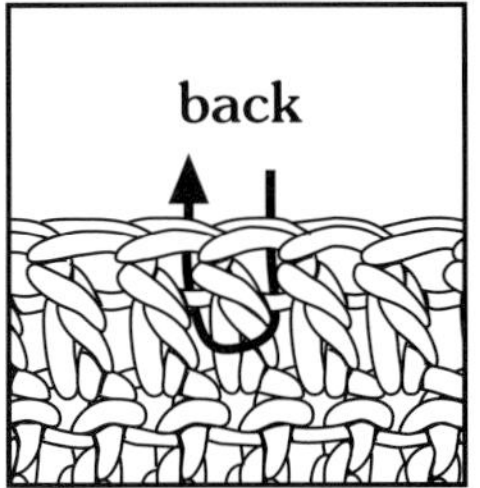

FRENCH KNOT

Using one strand of thread, work a French knot as indicated in pattern as follows: Bring needle up at 1. Wrap thread twice around needle and insert needle at 2, holding end of thread with non-stitching fingers ***(Fig. 5)***. Tighten knot; then pull needle through, holding thread until it must be released.

Fig. 5

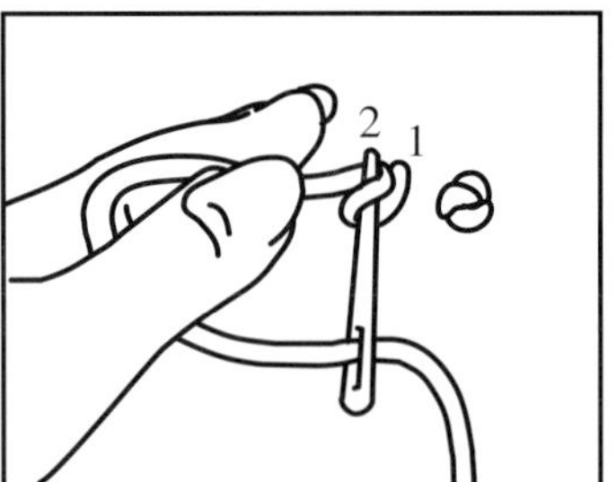

WASHING AND BLOCKING

For a more professional look, Doilies should be washed and blocked. Using a mild detergent and warm water and being careful not to rub, twist, or wring, gently squeeze suds through the piece. Rinse several times in cool, clear water. Roll piece in a clean terry towel and gently press out the excess moisture. Lay piece on a flat surface and shape to proper size; where needed, pin in place using rust-proof pins. Allow to dry **completely**.

1. ROSE BOUQUET

Shown on page 6.

Finished Size: $13^1/_4$" (33.5 cm) diameter

MATERIALS

Bedspread Weight Cotton Thread (size 10):
White - 110 yards (100.5 meters)
Red - 71 yards (65 meters)
Green - 17 yards (15.5 meters)
Steel crochet hooks, sizes 6 (1.80 mm) **and** 7 (1.65 mm) **or** sizes needed for gauge

GAUGE SWATCH: 3" (7.5 cm) diameter
Work same as Doily through Rnd 9.

STITCH GUIDE

BACK POST SINGLE CROCHET ***(abbreviated BPsc)***
Insert hook from **back** to **front** around post of st indicated ***(Fig. 4, page 3)***, YO and pull up a loop, YO and draw through both loops on hook.

ROSETTES (Make 6)

Rnd 1 (Right side)**:** With Red and using smaller size hook, ch 4, 9 dc in fourth ch from hook **(3 skipped chs counts as first dc)**; join with slip st to first dc: 10 dc.

Rnd 2: Ch 1, sc in same st and in each dc around; join with slip st to first sc.

Rnd 3: Ch 1, sc in same st, ch 3, skip next sc, ★ sc in next sc, ch 3, skip next sc; repeat from ★ around; join with slip st to first sc: 5 ch-3 sps.

Rnd 4: (Slip st, ch 2, 4 dc, ch 2, slip st) in first ch-3 sp and in each ch-3 sp around; do **not** join: 5 petals.

Rnd 5: Ch 1; working **behind** petals and in Back Loop Only of skipped sc on Rnd 2 ***(Fig. 1, page 3)***, (sc in next sc, ch 4) around; join with slip st to **both** loops of first sc: 5 ch-4 sps.

Rnd 6: (Slip st, ch 2, 6 dc, ch 2, slip st) in first ch-4 sp and in each ch-4 sp around; do **not** join: 5 petals.

Rnd 7: Ch 2; working **behind** petals and in ch-4 sps on Rnd 5, ★ skip first 3 dc on next petal, sc in sp **before** next dc, ch 5; repeat from ★ around; join with slip st to first sc: 5 ch-5 sps.

Rnd 8: (Slip st, ch 2, 8 dc, ch 2, slip st) in first ch-5 sp and in each ch-5 sp around; join with slip st to first slip st, finish off: 5 petals.

DOILY

With Red and using larger size hook, ch 6; join with slip st to form a ring.

Rnd 1 (Right side)**:** Ch 6 **(counts as first dc plus ch 3)**, (dc in ring, ch 3) 7 times; join with slip st to first dc: 8 dc and 8 ch-3 sps.

Rnd 2: Ch 1, (sc, hdc, 3 dc, hdc, sc) in first ch-3 sp and in each ch-3 sp around; join with slip st to first sc: 8 petals.

Rnd 3: Ch 1; working **behind** petals, work BPsc around first dc on Rnd 1, ch 4, (work BPsc around next dc on Rnd 1, ch 4) around; join with slip st to first BPsc: 8 ch-4 sps.

Rnd 4: Ch 1, (sc, hdc, 5 dc, hdc, sc) in first ch-4 sp and in each ch-4 sp around; join with slip st to first sc: 8 petals.

Rnd 5: Ch 1; working **behind** petals, work BPsc around first BPsc on Rnd 3, ch 5, (work BPsc around next BPsc on Rnd 3, ch 5) around; join with slip st to first BPsc: 8 ch-5 sps.

Rnd 6: Ch 1, (sc, hdc, 6 dc, hdc, sc) in first ch-5 sp and in each ch-5 sp around; join with slip st to first sc: 8 petals.

Rnd 7: Ch 1; working **behind** petals, work BPsc around first BPsc on Rnd 5, ch 6, (work BPsc around next BPsc on Rnd 5, ch 6) around; join with slip st to first BPsc, finish off: 8 ch-6 sps.

Rnd 8: With **right** side facing and using larger size hook, join Green with sc in any ch-6 sp ***(see Joining With Sc, page 3)***; ch 3, sc in same sp, ch 5, ★ (sc, ch 3, sc) in next ch-6 sp, ch 5; repeat from ★ around; join with slip st to first sc: 16 sps.

Rnd 9: (Slip st, ch 1, sc) in first ch-3 sp, 10 dc in next ch-5 sp, (sc in next ch-3 sp, 10 dc in next ch-5 sp) around; join with slip st to first sc, finish off: 88 sts.

Rnd 10: With **right** side facing and using larger size hook, join White with sc in first dc of any 10-dc group; (ch 3, skip next 2 dc, sc in next dc) 3 times, skip next sc, ★ sc in next dc, (ch 3, skip next 2 dc, sc in next dc) 3 times, skip next sc; repeat from ★ around; join with slip st to first sc: 24 ch-3 sps.

Rnd 11: (Slip st, ch 1, sc) in first ch-3 sp, (ch 4, sc in next ch-3 sp) around, ch 1, dc in first sc to form last ch-4 sp.

Rnd 12: Ch 1, sc in last ch-4 sp made, (ch 4, sc in next ch-4 sp) around, ch 1, dc in first sc to form last ch-4 sp.

Continued on page 5.

Rnd 13: Ch 1, sc in last ch-4 sp made, (ch 5, sc in next ch-4 sp) around, ch 2, dc in first sc to form last ch-5 sp.

Rnd 14: Ch 1, sc in last ch-5 sp made, (ch 6, sc in next ch-5 sp) around, ch 3, dc in first sc to form last ch-6 sp.

Rnd 15: Ch 1, sc in last ch-6 sp made, ch 6, (sc in next ch-6 sp, ch 6) around; join with slip st to first sc.

Rnd 16: Slip st in first ch, ch 3 **(counts as first dc, now and throughout)**, dc in same ch, 2 dc in each of next 5 chs, sc in next ch-6 sp, skip next sc, ★ 2 dc in each of next 6 chs, sc in next ch-6 sp, skip next sc; repeat from ★ around; join with slip st to first dc: 156 sts.

Rnd 17: Slip st in next 2 dc, ch 1, sc in same st, ★ † ch 3, skip next 2 dc, sc in next dc, ch 3, sc in next dc, ch 3, skip next 2 dc, sc in next dc †, ch 10, skip next 5 sts, sc in next dc; repeat from ★ 10 times **more**, then repeat from † to † once, ch 7, dc in first sc to form last loop: 36 ch-3 sps and 12 loops.

Rnd 18: Ch 3, dc in top of last dc made, 2 dc in side of joining dc, ch 2, skip next ch-3 sp, sc in next ch-3 sp, ★ ch 2, skip next ch-3 sp and first ch of next loop, 2 dc in each of next 8 chs, ch 2, skip next ch-3 sp, sc in next ch-3 sp; repeat from ★ around to last ch-3 sp, ch 2, skip last ch-3 sp and first ch of next loop, 2 dc in each of last 6 chs; join with slip st to first dc: 204 sts and 24 ch-2 sps.

Rnd 19: Ch 1, sc in same st, ch 7, skip next 2 ch-2 sps and next 3 dc, sc in next dc, ★ (ch 3, skip next 2 dc, sc in next dc) 3 times, ch 7, skip next 2 ch-2 sps and next 3 dc, sc in next dc; repeat from ★ around to last 8 dc, ch 3, skip next 2 dc, (sc in next dc, ch 3, skip next 2 dc) twice; join with slip st to first sc: 48 sps.

Rnd 20: (Slip st, ch 3, dc) in first ch, 2 dc in each of next 6 chs, sc in next ch-3 sp, (ch 3, sc in next ch-3 sp) twice, skip next sc, ★ 2 dc in each of next 7 chs, sc in next ch-3 sp, (ch 3, sc in next ch-3 sp) twice, skip next sc; repeat from ★ around; join with slip st to first dc: 168 dc and 24 ch-3 sps.

Rnd 21 (Joining rnd)**:** Ch 1, sc in same st, ★ † (ch 3, skip next dc, sc in next dc) 3 times, slip st in next 7 dc, ch 3, sc in next ch-3 sp, ch 1; holding Rosette with **wrong** side facing and working in ch-5 sps on Rnd 7, slip st in sp **between** center dc of any petal, ch 1, sc in next ch-3 sp on Rnd 20 of Doily, ch 3, skip next sc, slip st in next 7 dc, sc in next dc, (ch 3, skip next dc, sc in next dc) 3 times †, ch 8, skip next 2 ch-3 sps and next sc, sc in next dc; repeat from ★ 4 times **more**, then repeat from † to † once, ch 5, skip last 2 ch-3 sps and last sc, dc in first sc to form last ch-8 sp: 60 sps.

Rnd 22: Ch 3, dc in top of last dc made, work 4 dc evenly spaced across side of joining dc, ★ † sc in next ch-3 sp, (ch 3, sc in next ch-3 sp) twice, ch 4, working into ch-5 sps on Rnd 7 of next Rosette, slip st in sp between center dc of next petal, (ch 5, slip st in sp between center dc of next petal) 3 times, ch 4, sc in first ch-3 sp after slip sts on Rnd 21 of Doily, (ch 3, sc in next ch-3 sp) twice, skip next sc †, 2 dc in each of next 8 chs; repeat from ★ 4 times **more**, then repeat from † to † once, 2 dc in each of last 5 chs; join with slip st to first dc: 96 dc and 54 sps.

Rnd 23: Slip st in next 2 dc, ch 1, sc in same st, (ch 3, sc in next sp) 3 times, ★ † ch 4, sc in next ch-5 sp, ch 4, (sc, ch 3, sc) in next ch-5 sp, (ch 4, sc in next sp) twice, ch 3, (sc in next ch-3 sp, ch 3) twice, skip next 4 sts, sc in next dc †, (ch 3, skip next 2 dc, sc in next dc) 3 times, (ch 3, sc in next sp) 3 times; repeat from ★ 4 times **more**, then repeat from † to † once, (ch 3, skip next 2 dc, sc in next dc) twice, ch 1, skip last 2 sts, hdc in first sc to form last ch-3 sp: 84 sps.

Rnd 24: Ch 1, sc in last ch-3 sp made, (ch 4, sc in next sp) 4 times, ch 5, sc in next ch-4 sp, ch 5, (sc, ch 5) twice in next ch-3 sp, sc in next ch-4 sp, ch 5, ★ sc in next ch-4 sp, (ch 4, sc in next sp) 10 times, ch 5, sc in next ch-4 sp, ch 5, (sc, ch 5) twice in next ch-3 sp, sc in next ch-4 sp, ch 5; repeat from ★ around to last 6 sps, (sc in next sp, ch 4) 6 times; join with slip st to first sc: 90 sps.

Rnd 25: (Slip st, ch 1, sc) in first ch-4 sp, ch 5, sc in next ch-4 sp, ch 10, skip next 2 ch-4 sps, sc in next ch-5 sp, ch 5, sc in next ch-5 sp, ch 10, skip next ch-5 sp, ★ sc in next ch-5 sp, ch 5, sc in next ch-5 sp, ch 10, (skip next 2 ch-4 sps, sc in next sp, ch 5, sc in next sp, ch 10) 3 times, skip next ch-5 sp; repeat from ★ 4 times **more**, (sc in next sp, ch 5, sc in next sp, ch 10, skip next 2 ch-4 sps) twice; join with slip st to first sc: 24 ch-5 sps and 24 loops.

Rnd 26: Slip st in next 2 chs, ch 1, sc in same ch-5 sp, skip next sc, (dc in next ch, 2 dc in next ch) 5 times, ★ sc in next ch-5 sp, skip next sc, (dc in next ch, 2 dc in next ch) 5 times; repeat from ★ around; join with slip st to first sc, finish off: 384 sts.

Rnd 27: With **right** side facing and using larger size hook, join Green with sc in next dc; ★ † ch 3, skip next 2 dc, sc in next dc, ch 3, skip next 3 dc, (sc, ch 3) twice in next dc, skip next 3 dc, sc in next dc, ch 3, skip next 2 dc, sc in next dc, skip next sc †, sc in next dc; repeat from ★ 22 times **more**, then repeat from † to † once; join with slip st to first sc, finish off.

See Washing and Blocking, page 3.

1

2. ENGLISH GARDEN

Shown on Front Cover.

Finished Size: $12^{1}/_{4}$" (31 cm) diameter

MATERIALS

Bedspread Weight Cotton Thread (size 10):
- White - 96 yards (88 meters)
- Green - 17 yards (15.5 meters)
- Pink - 15 yards (13.5 meters)
- Lavender - 15 yards (13.5 meters)
- Blue - 15 yards (13.5 meters)
- Yellow - small amount

Steel crochet hook, size 6 (1.80 mm) **or** size needed for gauge

Tapestry needle

GAUGE SWATCH: $2^{1}/_{2}$" (6.5 cm) diameter
Work same as Doily through Rnd 5.

FLOWER CLUSTER (Make 10)

FIRST FLOWER

With Lavender, ch 3, (2 dc, ch 2, slip st) in third ch from hook, place marker around first dc made to mark **right** side and First Flower, (ch 2, 2 dc, ch 2, slip st) 4 times in same st; finish off: 5 petals.

SECOND FLOWER

With Blue, ch 3, (2 dc, ch 2, slip st) in third ch from hook, mark first dc as **right** side, (ch 2, 2 dc, ch 2, slip st) 3 times in same st, ch 2, dc in same st; with **wrong** side of First Flower facing, slip st in sp between center dc of any petal, (dc, ch 2, slip st) in same st on Second Flower; finish off: 5 petals.

THIRD FLOWER

With Pink, ch 3, (2 dc, ch 2, slip st) in third ch from hook, mark first dc as **right** side, (ch 2, 2 dc, ch 2, slip st) twice in same st, ch 2, dc in same st; with **wrong** side of First Flower facing, slip st in sp between center dc of petal (before petal joining), (dc, ch 2, slip st, ch 2, dc) in same st on Third Flower, with **wrong** side of Second Flower facing, slip st in sp between center dc of petal (after petal joining), (dc, ch 2, slip st) in same st on Third Flower; finish off: 5 petals.

With Yellow and using photo as a guide for placement, add a French Knot to center of each Flower *(Fig. 5, page 3)*.

DOILY

Rnd 1 (Right side)**:** With White, ch 4, 19 dc in fourth ch from hook **(3 skipped chs count as first dc)**; join with slip st to first dc: 20 dc.

Note: Loop a short piece of thread around any stitch to mark Rnd 1 as **right** side.

Rnd 2: Ch 4 **(counts as first dc plus ch 1)**, (dc in next dc, ch 1) around; join with slip st to first dc.

Rnd 3: Ch 1, sc in same st, (ch 3, sc in next dc) around, ch 1, hdc in first sc to form last ch-3 sp: 20 ch-3 sps.

Rnd 4: Ch 1, sc in last ch-3 sp made, (ch 3, sc in next ch-3 sp) around, ch 1, hdc in first sc to form last ch-3 sp.

Rnd 5: Ch 1, sc in last ch-3 sp made, (ch 4, sc in next ch-3 sp) around, ch 1, dc in first sc to form last ch-4 sp.

Rnd 6: Ch 1, sc in last ch-4 sp made, ch 5, (sc in next ch-4 sp, ch 5) around; join with slip st to first sc.

Rnd 7: Slip st in first ch-5 sp, ch 3 **(counts as first dc)**, 7 dc in same sp, (sc, ch 3, sc) in next ch-5 sp, ★ 8 dc in next ch-5 sp, (sc, ch 3, sc) in next ch-5 sp; repeat from ★ around; join with slip st to first dc: 80 dc.

Rnd 8: Ch 1, sc in same st, ch 3, skip next dc, sc in next dc, ch 3, skip next 2 dc, sc in next dc, ch 3, skip next dc, sc in next dc, ch 4, skip next 2 sc, ★ sc in next dc, ch 3, skip next dc, sc in next dc, ch 3, skip next 2 dc, sc in next dc, ch 3, skip next dc, sc in next dc, ch 4, skip next 2 sc; repeat from ★ around; join with slip st to first sc: 40 sps.

Rnd 9: (Slip st, ch 1, sc) in first ch-3 sp, (ch 3, sc in next sp) around, ch 1, hdc in first sc to form last ch-3 sp.

Rnd 10: Ch 1, sc in last ch-3 sp made, (ch 4, sc in next ch-3 sp) around, ch 1, dc in first sc to form last ch-4 sp.

Rnds 11 and 12: Ch 1, sc in last ch-4 sp made, (ch 4, sc in next ch-4 sp) around, ch 1, dc in first sc to form last ch-4 sp.

Rnd 13: Ch 1, sc in last ch-4 sp made, (ch 5, sc in next ch-4 sp) around, ch 2, dc in first sc to form last ch-5 sp.

Rnd 14 (Joining rnd)**:** Ch 1, sc in last ch-5 sp made, ★ † ch 5, sc in next ch-5 sp, ch 2; with **wrong** side of next Flower Cluster facing, slip st in sp between center dc of petal on First Flower (before petal joining), ch 2, sc in next ch-5 sp on Rnd 13 of Doily, ch 5, sc in next ch-5 sp, ch 2, slip st in sp between center dc of petal on Third Flower (after petal joining), ch 2 †, sc in next ch-5 sp on Doily; repeat from ★ 8 times **more**, then repeat from † to † once; join with slip st to first sc, finish off: 20 ch-5 sps.

Rnd 15 (leaves)**:** ★ † With Green, ch 5, slip st in second ch from hook, hdc in next ch, dc in next ch, 2 dc in next ch; with **wrong** side of Doily facing, slip st in next ch-5 sp between Flower Clusters; working in free loops of beginning ch ***(Fig. 3, page 3)***, 2 dc in first ch, hdc in next ch, sc in next ch, slip st in next ch †, finish off; repeat from ★ 8 times **more**, then repeat from † to † once, do **not** finish off: 10 leaves made.

Rnd 16: Ch 1, sc in ch at tip of same leaf, ★ † ch 3, skip next petal on First Flower, (sc, ch 3, sc) in sp between center dc of next petal, ch 5, skip next petal joining, **[**(sc, ch 3, sc) in sp between center dc of next petal on Second Flower, ch 5**]** 3 times, skip next petal joining, (sc, ch 3, sc) in sp between center dc of next petal on Third Flower, ch 3 †, sc in ch at tip of next leaf; repeat from ★ 8 times **more**, then repeat from † to † once; join with slip st to first sc: 110 sps.

Rnd 17: Ch 1, (sc, ch 3, sc) in same st, ch 5, skip next 2 ch-3 sps, (sc, ch 3, sc) in next ch-5 sp, ch 5, **[**skip next ch-3 sp, (sc, ch 3, sc) in next ch-5 sp, ch 5**]** 3 times, skip next 2 ch-3 sps, ★ (sc, ch 3, sc) in next sc, ch 5, skip next 2 ch-3 sps, (sc, ch 3, sc) in next ch-5 sp, ch 5, **[**skip next ch-3 sp, (sc, ch 3, sc) in next ch-5 sp, ch 5**]** 3 times, skip next 2 ch-3 sps; repeat from ★ around; join with slip st to first sc, finish off: 100 sps.

Rnd 18: With **right** side facing, join White with sc in first ch-5 sp after joining ***(see Joining With Sc, page 3)***; ch 5, **[**skip next ch-3 sp, (sc, ch 3, sc) in next ch-5 sp, ch 5**]** 3 times, ★ (skip next ch-3 sp, sc in next ch-5 sp, ch 5) twice, **[**skip next ch-3 sp, (sc, ch 3, sc) in next ch-5 sp, ch 5**]** 3 times; repeat from ★ around to last 3 sps, skip next ch-3 sp, sc in next ch-5 sp, ch 2, skip last ch-3 sp, dc in first sc to form last ch-5 sp: 80 sps.

Rnd 19: Ch 1, sc in last ch-5 sp made, ch 3, (sc, ch 3, sc) in next ch-5 sp, ★ † ch 5, skip next ch-3 sp, **[**(sc, ch 3, sc) in next sp, ch 5**]** 3 times, skip next ch-3 sp, (sc, ch 3, sc) in next ch-5 sp †, (ch 3, sc) twice in next 2 ch-5 sps; repeat from ★ 8 times **more**, then repeat from † to † once, ch 3, sc in same sp as first sc, ch 3; join with slip st to first sc: 120 sps.

Rnd 20: (Slip st, ch 1, sc) in first ch-3 sp, ★ † ch 3, skip next ch-3 sp, (sc, ch 3, sc) in next ch-5 sp, **[**ch 5, skip next ch-3 sp, (sc, ch 3, sc) in next ch-5 sp**]** 3 times, ch 3, skip next ch-3 sp, sc in next ch-3 sp †, ch 5, skip next ch-3 sp, sc in next ch-3 sp; repeat from ★ 8 times **more**, then repeat from † to † once, ch 2, skip last ch-3 sp, dc in first sc to form last ch-5 sp: 100 sps.

Rnd 21: Ch 1, sc in last ch-5 sp made, ch 3, ★ † sc in next ch-3 sp, ch 5, skip next ch-3 sp, **[**(sc, ch 3, sc) in next ch-5 sp, ch 5, skip next ch-3 sp**]** 3 times, sc in next ch-3 sp, ch 3 †, (sc, ch 3) twice in next ch-5 sp; repeat from ★ 8 times **more**, then repeat from † to † once, sc in same sp as first sc, ch 1, hdc in first sc to form last ch-3 sp.

Rnd 22: Ch 6, dc in last ch-3 sp made, ch 3, ★ † skip next ch-3 sp, (sc, ch 3, sc) in next ch-5 sp, **[**ch 5, skip next ch-3 sp, (sc, ch 3, sc) in next ch-5 sp**]** 3 times, ch 3, skip next ch-3 sp †, (dc, ch 3) twice in next ch-3 sp; repeat from ★ 8 times **more**, then repeat from † to † once; join with slip st to third ch of beginning ch-6, finish off.

See Washing and Blocking, page 3.

3

6
7

3. FORGET-ME-NOTS

Shown on page 9.

Finished Size: $10^1/_2$" (26.5 cm) diameter

MATERIALS

Bedspread Weight Cotton Thread (size 10):
White - 110 yards (100.5 meters)
Blue - 52 yards (47.5 meters)
Yellow - 39 yards (35.5 meters)
Green - 18 yards (16.5 meters)
Steel crochet hook, size 6 (1.80 mm) **or** size needed for gauge

GAUGE SWATCH: 2" (5 cm) diameter
Work same as Doily through Rnd 5.

STITCH GUIDE

DOUBLE TREBLE CROCHET ***(abbreviated dtr)***
YO 3 times, insert hook in ch-3 sp indicated, YO and pull up a loop (5 loops on hook), (YO and draw through 2 loops on hook) 4 times.

POPCORN
3 Dc in st indicated, drop loop from hook, insert hook in first dc of 3-dc group, hook dropped loop and draw through.

FLOWER (Make 18)

Rnd 1 (center)**:** With Yellow, ch 4, 2 dc in fourth ch from hook **(3 skipped chs count as first dc)**, place marker around last dc made to mark **right** side, drop loop from hook, insert hook in first dc, hook dropped loop and draw through (beginning Popcorn made), ch 1, (work Popcorn in same ch, ch 1) 5 times; join with slip st to top of beginning Popcorn, finish off: 6 ch-1 sps.

Rnd 2: With **right** side facing, join Blue with slip st in any ch-1 sp; (ch 2, 4 dc, ch 2, slip st) in same sp, (slip st, ch 2, 4 dc, ch 2, slip st) in next ch-1 sp and in each ch-1 sp around; join with slip st to first slip st: 6 petals.

Rnd 3: Ch 1; working **behind** petals and in ch-1 sps on center, ★ skip first 2 dc on next petal, sc in sp **before** next dc, ch 3; repeat from ★ around; join with slip st to first sc, finish off: 6 ch-3 sps.

Leaves: With **right** side facing, join Green with slip st in any ch-3 sp; ch 5, working in back ridge of chs ***(Fig. 2, page 3)***, slip st in second ch from hook, sc in next ch, dc in last 2 chs, (slip st, ch 2, slip st) in next ch-3 sp, ch 5, working in back ridge of chs, slip st in second ch from hook, sc in next ch, dc in last 2 chs, slip st in next ch-3 sp; finish off.

DOILY

Rnds 1-3: Work same as Flower: 6 ch-3 sps.

Rnd 4: With **right** side facing, join White with dc in any ch-3 sp ***(see Joining With Dc, page 3)***; 5 dc in same sp, 6 dc in next ch-3 sp and in each ch-3 sp around; join with slip st to first dc: 36 dc.

Rnd 5: Ch 3 **(counts as first dc, now and throughout)**, dc in same st and in next dc, (2 dc in next dc, dc in next dc) around; join with slip st to first dc, finish off: 54 dc.

Rnd 6: With **right** side facing, join Green with sc in same st as joining ***(see Joining With Sc, page 3)***; ch 1, (sc in next dc, ch 1) around; join with slip st to first sc, finish off.

Rnd 7: With **right** side facing, join White with sc in any sc; ★ ch 3, skip next sc, sc in next sc; repeat from ★ around to last sc, ch 1, skip last sc, hdc in first sc to form last ch-3 sp: 27 ch-3 sps.

Rnds 8 and 9: Ch 1, sc in last ch-3 sp made, (ch 3, sc in next ch-3 sp) around, ch 1, hdc in first sc to form last ch-3 sp.

Rnd 10: Ch 1, sc in last ch-3 sp made, (ch 4, sc in next ch-3 sp) around, ch 1, dc in first sc to form last ch-4 sp.

Rnd 11: Ch 1, sc in last ch-4 sp made, 11 dc in next ch-4 sp, sc in next ch-4 sp, ★ ch 3, sc in next ch-4 sp, 11 dc in next ch-4 sp, sc in next ch-4 sp; repeat from ★ around, ch 1, hdc in first sc to form last ch-3 sp: 99 dc and 9 ch-3 sps.

Rnd 12: Ch 1, sc in last ch-3 sp made, ch 3, skip next 3 sts, sc in next dc, (ch 3, skip next 2 dc, sc in next dc) twice, ★ ch 3, sc in next ch-3 sp, ch 3, skip next 3 sts, sc in next dc, (ch 3, skip next 2 dc, sc in next dc) twice; repeat from ★ around, ch 1, hdc in first sc to form last ch-3 sp: 36 ch-3 sps.

Rnd 13: Ch 1, sc in last ch-3 sp made, (ch 4, sc in next ch-3 sp) around, ch 1, dc in first sc to form last ch-4 sp.

Rnd 14: Ch 1, sc in last ch-4 sp made, (ch 4, sc in next ch-4 sp) around, ch 2, hdc in first sc to form last ch-4 sp.

Rnd 15: Ch 3, 4 dc in last ch-4 sp made, sc in next ch-4 sp, (11 dc in next ch-4 sp, sc in next ch-4 sp) around, 6 dc in same sp as first dc; join with slip st to first dc: 216 sts.

Rnd 16: Ch 1, sc in same st, ch 7, skip next 9 sts, sc in next dc, ★ ch 3, skip next dc, sc in next dc, ch 7, skip next 9 sts, sc in next dc; repeat from ★ around to last dc, ch 1, skip last dc, hdc in first sc to form last ch-3 sp: 36 sps.

Rnd 17: Ch 1, sc in last ch-3 sp made, skip next sc, 2 dc in next ch, (dc in next ch, 2 dc in next ch) 3 times, ★ sc in next ch-3 sp, skip next sc, 2 dc in next ch, (dc in next ch, 2 dc in next ch) 3 times; repeat from ★ around; join with slip st to first sc: 216 sts.

Rnd 18 (Joining rnd)**:** Slip st in next 3 dc, ch 1, sc in same st, ★ † ch 3, skip next dc, sc in next dc, ch 1; with **wrong** side of next Flower facing, slip st in ch-2 sp between Leaves, ch 1, skip next dc on Rnd 17 of Doily, sc in next dc, ch 3, skip next dc, sc in next dc †, ch 3, skip next 5 sts, sc in next dc; repeat from ★ 16 times **more**, then repeat from † to † once, ch 1, skip last 5 sts, hdc in first sc to form last ch-3 sp.

Rnd 19: Ch 5 **(counts as first dtr)**, 7 dc in each of next 3 ch-3 sps on Rnd 3 of next Flower, skip next ch-3 sp on Rnd 18 of Doily, ★ dtr in next ch-3 sp, 7 dc in each of next 3 ch-3 sps on Rnd 3 of next Flower, skip next ch-3 sp on Rnd 18 of Doily; repeat from ★ around; join with slip st to first dtr: 378 dc.

Rnd 20: Slip st in next 3 dc, ch 1, sc in same st, (ch 3, skip next dc, sc in next dc) 8 times, skip next 5 sts, ★ sc in next dc, (ch 3, skip next dc, sc in next dc) 8 times, skip next 5 sts; repeat from ★ around; join with slip st to first sc: 144 ch-3 sps.

Rnd 21: (Slip st, ch 1, sc) in first ch-3 sp, ch 3, (sc in next ch-3 sp, ch 3) 6 times, ★ sc in next 2 ch-3 sps, ch 3, (sc in next ch-3 sp, ch 3) 6 times; repeat from ★ around to last ch-3 sp, sc in last ch-3 sp; join with slip st to first sc, finish off.

See Washing and Blocking, page 3.

4. DAISY DELIGHT

Shown on Back Cover.

Finished Size: 13" (33 cm) diameter

MATERIALS

Bedspread Weight Cotton Thread (size 10):
- White - 184 yards (168 meters)
- Green - 28 yards (25.5 meters)
- Yellow - 14 yards (13 meters)

Steel crochet hook, size 6 (1.80 mm) **or** size needed for gauge

GAUGE SWATCH: 2¾" (7 cm) diameter
Work same as Doily through Rnd 7.

STITCH GUIDE

TREBLE CROCHET ***(abbreviated tr)***
YO twice, insert hook in st or sp indicated, YO and pull up a loop (4 loops on hook), (YO and draw through 2 loops on hook) 3 times.

2-TR CLUSTER (uses one ch-3 sp)
★ YO twice, insert hook in ch-3 sp indicated, YO and pull up a loop, (YO and draw through 2 loops on hook) twice; repeat from ★ once more, YO and draw through all 3 loops on hook.

3-TR CLUSTER (uses one ch-3 sp)
★ YO twice, insert hook in ch-3 sp indicated, YO and pull up a loop, (YO and draw through 2 loops on hook) twice; repeat from ★ 2 times more, YO and draw through all 4 loops on hook.

SHELL
(2 Dc, ch 2, 2 dc) in ch-3 sp indicated.

PICOT
Ch 1, slip st in top of last tr made.

DAISY (Make 9)

Rnd 1 (Right side)**:** With Yellow, ch 2, 8 sc in second ch from hook; join with slip st to first sc.

Note: Loop a short piece of thread around any stitch to mark Rnd 1 as **right** side.

Rnds 2 and 3: Ch 1, sc in same st and in each sc around; join with slip st to first sc.

Finish off.

Continued on page 13.

Rnd 4: With **right** side facing and working in Back Loops Only ***(Fig. 1, page 3)***, join White with slip st in any sc; ch 3, (tr, work Picot, tr, ch 3, slip st) in same st, (slip st, ch 3, tr, work Picot, tr, ch 3, slip st) in next sc and in each sc around; join with slip st to **both** loops of first slip st: 8 petals.

Rnd 5: Ch 1; working **behind** petals and in same sc on Rnd 3, (sc in sp between center tr of next petal, ch 3) around; join with slip st to first sc, finish off: 8 ch-3 sps.

Rnd 6: With **right** side facing, join Green with slip st in any ch-3 sp; ch 3, work 2-tr Cluster in same sp, (ch 5, work 3-tr Cluster in next ch-3 sp) 6 times, leave remaining ch-3 sp unworked; finish off: 6 ch-5 sps.

DOILY

Rnds 1-5: Work same as Daisy: 8 ch-3 sps.

Rnd 6: With **right** side facing, join Green with slip st in any ch-3 sp; ch 3, work 2-tr Cluster in same sp, ch 5, (work 3-tr Cluster in next ch-3 sp, ch 5) around; join with slip st to top of first 2-tr Cluster, finish off: 8 ch-5 sps.

Rnd 7: With **right** side facing, join White with dc in any ch-5 sp ***(see Joining With Dc, page 3)***; 8 dc in same sp, sc in next Cluster, (9 dc in next ch-5 sp, sc in next Cluster) around; join with slip st to first dc: 80 sts.

Rnd 8: Ch 1, sc in same st, (ch 3, skip next dc, sc in next dc) 4 times, skip next sc, ★ sc in next dc, (ch 3, skip next dc, sc in next dc) 4 times, skip next sc; repeat from ★ around; join with slip st to first sc: 32 ch-3 sps.

Rnd 9: (Slip st, ch 1, sc) in first ch-3 sp, (ch 3, sc in next ch-3 sp) around, ch 1, hdc in first sc to form last ch-3 sp.

Rnd 10: Ch 1, sc in last ch-3 sp made, work Shell in next ch-3 sp, (sc in next ch-3 sp, work Shell in next ch-3 sp) around; join with slip st to first sc: 16 sc and 16 ch-2 sps.

Rnd 11: Ch 1, sc in same st, ch 1, 7 dc in next ch-2 sp, ch 1, skip next 2 dc, ★ sc in next sc, ch 1, 7 dc in next ch-2 sp, ch 1, skip next 2 dc; repeat from ★ around; join with slip st to first sc: 128 sts and 32 ch-1 sps.

Rnd 12: Slip st in next ch and in next dc, ch 1, sc in same st, (ch 3, skip next dc, sc in next dc) 3 times, skip next sc, ★ sc in next dc, (ch 3, skip next dc, sc in next dc) 3 times, skip next sc; repeat from ★ around; join with slip st to first sc: 48 ch-3 sps.

Rnds 13 and 14: Repeat Rnds 9 and 10: 24 sc and 24 ch-2 sps.

Rnd 15: Ch 1, sc in same st, 7 dc in next ch-2 sp, skip next 2 dc, ★ sc in next sc, 7 dc in next ch-2 sp, skip next 2 dc; repeat from ★ around; join with slip st to first sc: 192 sts.

Rnd 16: (Slip st, ch 1, sc) in next dc, (ch 3, skip next dc, sc in next dc) 3 times, skip next sc, ★ sc in next dc, (ch 3, skip next dc, sc in next dc) 3 times, skip next sc; repeat from ★ around; join with slip st to first sc: 72 ch-3 sps.

Rnd 17: (Slip st, ch 1, sc) in first ch-3 sp, (ch 3, sc in next ch-3 sp) around, ch 1, hdc in first sc to form last ch-3 sp.

Rnd 18 (Joining rnd)**:** Ch 1, sc in last ch-3 sp made, (work Shell in next ch-3 sp, sc in next ch-3 sp) twice, ★ † ch 1; with **wrong** side of Daisy facing, slip st in unworked ch-3 sp on Rnd 5, ch 1, sc in same sp on Doily as last sc made †, (work Shell in next ch-3 sp, sc in next ch-3 sp) 4 times; repeat from ★ 7 times **more**, then repeat from † to † once, work Shell in next ch-3 sp, sc in next ch-3 sp, work Shell in last ch-3 sp; join with slip st to first sc: 36 ch-2 sps.

Rnd 19: Slip st in next 2 dc and in next ch-2 sp, ch 1, sc in same sp, ★ † 7 dc in first ch-5 sp on Rnd 6 of next Daisy, (sc in next 3-tr Cluster, 7 dc in next ch-5 sp) 5 times, skip next joining and next ch-2 sp, sc in next ch-2 sp on Rnd 18 of Doily, ch 3 †, sc in next ch-2 sp; repeat from ★ 7 times **more**, then repeat from † to † once; join with slip st to first sc: 378 dc.

Rnd 20: Slip st in next 5 dc, ch 1, sc in same st, ★ † ch 3, (skip next st, sc in next dc) twice, **[**(ch 3, skip next dc, sc in next dc) 3 times, skip next sc, sc in next dc**]** 4 times, ch 3, skip next dc, sc in next dc, ch 1, skip next ch-3 sp and first 4 dc on next 7-dc group †, sc in next dc; repeat from ★ 7 times **more**, then repeat from † to † once; join with slip st to first sc: 126 ch-3 sps.

Rnd 21: (Slip st, ch 1, sc) in first ch-3 sp, (ch 4, sc in next ch-3 sp) 13 times, skip next ch-1 sp, ★ sc in next ch-3 sp, (ch 4, sc in next ch-3 sp) 13 times, skip next ch-1 sp; repeat from ★ around; join with slip st to first sc: 117 ch-4 sps.

Rnd 22: (Slip st, ch 1, sc) in first ch-4 sp, ★ † (ch 4, sc in next ch-4 sp) 5 times, ch 1, (2 tr, ch 3, 2 tr) in next ch-4 sp, ch 1, (sc in next ch-4 sp, ch 4) 5 times †, sc in each of next 2 ch-4 sps; repeat from ★ 7 times **more**, then repeat from † to † once, sc in last ch-4 sp; join with slip st to first sc, finish off.

See Washing and Blocking, page 3.

5. SWEET VIOLETS

Shown on page 2.

Finished Size: $13^1/_2$" (34.5 cm) diameter

MATERIALS

Bedspread Weight Cotton Thread (size 10):
White - 130 yards (119 meters)
Purple - 30 yards (27.5 meters)
Green - 24 yards (22 meters)
Yellow - small amount
Steel crochet hook, size 6 (1.80 mm) **or** size needed for gauge
Tapestry needle

GAUGE SWATCH: $2^1/_8$" (5.5 cm) diameter
Work same as Doily through Rnd 4.

VIOLET (Make 16)

With Purple, ch 4, (3 dc, ch 3, slip st) in fourth ch from hook, place marker around any dc to mark **right** side, (ch 3, 3 dc, ch 3, slip st) 4 times in same ch; finish off: 5 petals.

With Yellow and using photo as a guide for placement, add a French Knot to center of each petal ***(Fig. 5, page 3)***.

FIRST LEAF

With **right** side facing, join Green with slip st in third dc of any petal; ch 4, working in back ridge of chs ***(Fig. 2, page 3)***, sc in second ch from hook, hdc in next ch, dc in next ch; join with slip st to first dc of next petal, finish off.

SECOND LEAF

With **right** side facing, skip next petal and join Green with slip st in third dc of next petal; ch 4, working in back ridge of chs, sc in second ch from hook, hdc in next ch, dc in next ch; join with slip st to first dc of next petal, finish off.

DOILY

Rnd 1 (Right side)**:** With White, ch 4, 15 dc in fourth ch from hook **(3 skipped chs count as first dc)**; join with slip st to first dc: 16 dc.

Note: Loop a short piece of thread around any stitch to mark Rnd 1 as **right** side.

Rnd 2: Ch 3 **(counts as first dc, now and throughout)**, dc in same st, 2 dc in next dc and in each dc around; join with slip st to first dc: 32 dc.

Rnd 3: Ch 1, sc in same st, ch 3, skip next dc, ★ sc in next dc, ch 3, skip next dc; repeat from ★ around; join with slip st to first sc: 16 ch-3 sps.

Rnd 4: (Slip st, ch 3, dc, ch 2, 2 dc) in first ch-3 sp, (sc, ch 3, sc) in next ch-3 sp, ★ (2 dc, ch 2, 2 dc) in next ch-3 sp, (sc, ch 3, sc) in next ch-3 sp; repeat from ★ around; join with slip st to first dc.

Rnd 5: Slip st in next dc and in next ch-2 sp, ch 3, (dc, ch 2, 2 dc) in same sp, ch 1, (sc, ch 3, sc) in next ch-3 sp, ch 1, ★ (2 dc, ch 2, 2 dc) in next ch-2 sp, ch 1, (sc, ch 3, sc) in next ch-3 sp, ch 1; repeat from ★ around; join with slip st to first dc: 32 sps.

Rnd 6: Slip st in next dc and in next ch-2 sp, ch 3, (dc, ch 2, 2 dc) in same sp, ch 2, skip next ch-1 sp, (sc, ch 3, sc) in next ch-3 sp, ch 2, skip next ch-1 sp, ★ (2 dc, ch 2) twice in next ch-2 sp, skip next ch-1 sp, (sc, ch 3, sc) in next ch-3 sp, ch 2, skip next ch-1 sp; repeat from ★ around; join with slip st to first dc.

Rnd 7: Slip st in next dc and in next ch-2 sp, ch 3, (dc, ch 2, 2 dc) in same sp, ch 3, skip next ch-2 sp, (sc, ch 3) twice in next ch-3 sp, skip next ch-2 sp, ★ (2 dc, ch 2, 2 dc) in next ch-2 sp, ch 3, skip next ch-2 sp, (sc, ch 3) twice in next ch-3 sp, skip next ch-2 sp; repeat from ★ around; join with slip st to first dc.

Rnd 8 (Joining rnd)**:** Slip st in next dc and in next ch-2 sp, ch 3, (dc, ch 2, 2 dc) in same sp, ch 2; ★ † with **wrong** side of next Violet facing, slip st in center dc of same petal as First Leaf (after Leaf joining), ch 2, skip next ch-3 sp on Rnd 7 of Doily, (sc, ch 3, sc) in next ch-3 sp, ch 2, slip st in center dc of next petal (before joining of Second Leaf), ch 2, skip next ch-3 sp on Rnd 7 of Doily †, (2 dc, ch 2) twice in next ch-2 sp; repeat from ★ 6 times **more**, then repeat from † to † once; join with slip st to first dc: 8 Violets joined.

Rnd 9: Slip st in next dc and in next ch-2 sp, ch 3, (dc, ch 2, 2 dc) in same sp, ch 2, ★ † sc in center dc of next petal (after Leaf joining), (ch 5, sc in center dc of next petal) twice, ch 2 †, (2 dc, ch 2) twice in center ch-2 sp on Doily (between Violets); repeat from ★ 6 times **more**, then repeat from † to † once; join with slip st to first dc: 40 sps.

Rnd 10: Slip st in next dc and in next ch-2 sp, ch 3, [dc, (ch 2, 2 dc) twice] in same sp, ★ † ch 3, skip next ch-2 sp, (sc, ch 3, sc) in next ch-5 sp, ch 5, (sc, ch 3) twice in next ch-5 sp, skip next ch-2 sp †, 2 dc in next ch-2 sp, (ch 2, 2 dc in same sp) twice; repeat from ★ 6 times **more**, then repeat from † to † once; join with slip st to first dc: 56 sps.

Continued on page 15.

Rnd 11: Slip st in next dc and in next ch-2 sp, ch 3, (dc, ch 2, 2 dc) in same sp, ch 3, (2 dc, ch 2, 2 dc) in next ch-2 sp, ch 3, ★ † skip next ch-3 sp, sc in next ch-3 sp, skip next sc, 2 dc in each of next 5 chs, sc in next ch-3 sp, ch 3, skip next ch-3 sp †, **[**(2 dc, ch 2, 2 dc) in next ch-2 sp, ch 3**]** twice; repeat from ★ 6 times **more**, then repeat from † to † once; join with slip st to first dc: 144 dc and 40 sps.

Rnd 12: Slip st in next dc and in next ch-2 sp, ch 3, (dc, ch 2, 2 dc) in same sp, ★ † ch 3, sc in next ch-3 sp, ch 3, (2 dc, ch 2, 2 dc) in next ch-2 sp, ch 3, skip next ch-3 sp and next sc, sc in next dc, (ch 4, skip next 2 dc, sc in next dc) 3 times, ch 3, skip next ch-3 sp †, (2 dc, ch 2, 2 dc) in next ch-2 sp; repeat from ★ 6 times **more**, then repeat from † to † once; join with slip st to first dc: 72 sps.

Rnd 13: Slip st in next dc and in next ch-2 sp, ch 3, (dc, ch 2, 2 dc) in same sp, ★ † ch 3, (sc in next ch-3 sp, ch 3) twice, (2 dc, ch 2, 2 dc) in next ch-2 sp, ch 3, skip next ch-3 sp, sc in next ch-4 sp, (ch 4, sc in next ch-4 sp) twice, ch 3, skip next ch-3 sp †, (2 dc, ch 2, 2 dc) in next ch-2 sp; repeat from ★ 6 times **more**, then repeat from † to † once; join with slip st to first dc.

Rnd 14: Slip st in next dc and in next ch-2 sp, ch 3, (dc, ch 2, 2 dc) in same sp, ★ † ch 3, (sc in next ch-3 sp, ch 3) 3 times, (2 dc, ch 2, 2 dc) in next ch-2 sp, ch 3, skip next ch-3 sp, sc in next ch-4 sp, ch 4, sc in next ch-4 sp, ch 3, skip next ch-3 sp †, (2 dc, ch 2, 2 dc) in next ch-2 sp; repeat from ★ 6 times **more**, then repeat from † to † once; join with slip st to first dc.

Rnd 15: Slip st in next dc and in next ch-2 sp, ch 3, (dc, ch 2, 2 dc) in same sp, ★ † ch 3, (sc in next ch-3 sp, ch 3) 4 times, (2 dc, ch 2, 2 dc) in next ch-2 sp, ch 3, skip next ch-3 sp, sc in next ch-4 sp, ch 3, skip next ch-3 sp †, (2 dc, ch 2, 2 dc) in next ch-2 sp; repeat from ★ 6 times **more**, then repeat from † to † once; join with slip st to first dc.

Rnd 16 (Joining rnd)**:** Slip st in next dc and in next ch-2 sp, ch 3, (dc, ch 2, 2 dc) in same sp, ★ † (ch 3, sc in next ch-3 sp) twice, ch 1; with **wrong** side of Violet facing, slip st in center dc of same petal as First Leaf (after Leaf joining), ch 1, sc in next ch-3 sp on Rnd 15 of Doily, ch 1, slip st in center dc of next petal (before joining of Second Leaf), ch 1, (sc in next ch-3 sp on Rnd 15 of Doily, ch 3) twice, (2 dc, ch 2, 2 dc) in next ch-2 sp, ch 3, skip next ch-3 sp, slip st in next sc, ch 3, skip next ch-3 sp †, (2 dc, ch 2, 2 dc) in next ch-2 sp; repeat from ★ 6 times **more**, then repeat from † to † once; join with slip st to first dc, do **not** finish off: last 8 Violets joined.

FIRST POINT

Row 1: Slip st in next dc and in next ch-2 sp, ch 5, (2 dc, ch 2, 2 dc) in same sp, ch 1, sc in next ch-3 sp, ch 3, sc in center dc of next petal (after Leaf joining), ch 5, sc in first dc of next petal, ch 5, skip next dc, sc in next dc, ch 5, sc in center dc of next petal, ch 3, skip next ch-3 sp on Rnd 16 of Doily, sc in next ch-3 sp, ch 1, (2 dc, ch 2, 2 dc) in next ch-2 sp, leave remaining sts and sps unworked: 9 sps.

Row 2: Ch 5, turn; (2 dc, ch 2, 2 dc) in first ch-2 sp, ch 3, skip next 2 sps, sc in next ch-5 sp, (ch 5, sc in next ch-5 sp) twice, ch 3, skip next 2 sps, (2 dc, ch 2, 2 dc) in last ch-2 sp: 6 sps.

Row 3: Ch 5, turn; (2 dc, ch 2, 2 dc) in first ch-2 sp, ch 3, skip next ch-3 sp, sc in next ch-5 sp, ch 5, sc in next ch-5 sp, ch 3, skip next ch-3 sp, (2 dc, ch 2, 2 dc) in last ch-2 sp: 5 sps.

Row 4: Ch 5, turn; (2 dc, ch 2, 2 dc) in first ch-2 sp, ch 4, skip next ch-3 sp, sc in next ch-5 sp, ch 4, skip next ch-3 sp, (2 dc, ch 2, 2 dc) in last ch-2 sp: 4 sps.

Row 5: Ch 5, turn; (2 dc, ch 2, 2 dc) in first ch-2 sp, ch 3, skip next ch-4 sp, slip st in next sc, ch 3, skip next ch-4 sp, (2 dc, ch 2, 2 dc) in last ch-2 sp.

Row 6: Ch 5, turn; (2 dc, ch 2) twice in first ch-2 sp, skip next ch-3 sp, slip st in next slip st, ch 2, skip next ch-3 sp, (2 dc, ch 2, 2 dc) in last ch-2 sp.

Row 7: Ch 5, turn; pull up a loop in first ch-2 sp, skip next 2 ch-2 sps, pull up a loop in last ch-2 sp, YO and draw through all 3 loops on hook; finish off.

REMAINING 7 POINTS

Row 1: With **right** side facing, skip next 2 ch-3 sps on Rnd 16 of Doily and join White with slip st in next ch-2 sp; ch 5, (2 dc, ch 2, 2 dc) in same sp, ch 1, sc in next ch-3 sp, ch 3, sc in center dc of next petal (after Leaf joining), ch 5, sc in first dc of next petal, ch 5, skip next dc, sc in next dc, ch 5, sc in center dc of next petal, ch 3, skip next ch-3 sp on Rnd 16 of Doily, sc in next ch-3 sp, ch 1, (2 dc, ch 2, 2 dc) in next ch-2 sp, leave remaining sts and sps unworked: 9 sps.

Rows 2-7: Work same as First Point.

FILL-IN LEAF (Make 8)
With Green, ch 5, slip st in second ch from hook, sc in next ch, hdc in next ch, 5 dc in last ch; working in free loops of beginning ch ***(Fig. 3, page 3)***, hdc in next ch, sc in next ch, slip st in next ch; finish off.

Using photo as a guide for placement, sew each Fill-In Leaf to slip st on Rnd 16 (between Points).

See Washing and Blocking, page 3.

---

6. SUNFLOWERS

Shown on page 10.

Finished Size: 13" (33 cm) diameter

MATERIALS
Bedspread Weight Cotton Thread (size 10):
White - 66 yards (60.5 meters)
Green - 51 yards (46.5 meters)
Yellow - 29 yards (26.5 meters)
Brown - 8 yards (7.5 meters)
Steel crochet hooks, sizes 6 (1.80 mm) **and** 7 (1.65 mm) **or** sizes needed for gauge

GAUGE SWATCH: 2" (5 cm) diameter
Work same as Doily through Rnd 3.

STITCH GUIDE

TREBLE CROCHET ***(abbreviated tr)***
YO twice, insert hook in sc indicated, YO and pull up a loop (4 loops on hook), (YO and draw through 2 loops on hook) 3 times.

CLUSTER (uses one ch-5 sp)
★ YO, insert hook in ch-5 sp indicated, YO and pull up a loop, YO and draw through 2 loops on hook; repeat from ★ 2 times **more**, YO and draw through all 4 loops on hook.

PICOT
Ch 8, slip st in sixth ch from hook, ch 2.

DOILY

With White and using larger size hook, ch 4; join with slip st to form a ring.

Rnd 1 (Right side)**:** Ch 1, 16 sc in ring; join with slip st to first sc.

Note: Loop a short piece of thread around any stitch to mark Rnd 1 as **right** side.

Rnd 2: Ch 3 **(counts as first dc)**, dc in same st, 2 dc in next sc and in each sc around; join with slip st to first dc: 32 dc.

Rnd 3: Ch 4 **(counts as first dc plus ch 1)**, (dc in next dc, ch 1) around; join with slip st to first dc: 32 ch-1 sps.

Rnd 4: (Slip st, ch 1, sc) in first ch-1 sp, (ch 3, sc in next ch-1 sp) around, ch 1, hdc in first sc to form last ch-3 sp.

Rnds 5-8: Ch 1, sc in last ch-3 sp made, (ch 3, sc in next ch-3 sp) around, ch 1, hdc in first sc to form last ch-3 sp.

Rnd 9: Ch 1, sc in last ch-3 sp made, (ch 4, sc in next ch-3 sp) around, ch 1, dc in first sc to form last ch-4 sp.

Rnd 10: Ch 1, sc in last ch-4 sp made, ch 5, (sc in next ch-4 sp, ch 5) around; join with slip st to first sc, finish off.

Rnd 11: With **right** side facing and using larger size hook, join Green with sc in any ch-5 sp ***(see Joining With Sc, page 3)***; ch 4, (work Cluster, ch 4) twice in next ch-5 sp, ★ sc in next ch-5 sp, ch 4, (work Cluster, ch 4) twice in next ch-5 sp; repeat from ★ around; join with slip st to first sc, finish off: 48 ch-4 sps.

Rnd 12: With **right** side facing and using larger size hook, join White with sc in any ch-4 sp between 2 Clusters; (ch 4, sc in next ch-4 sp) around, ch 1, dc in first sc to form last ch-4 sp.

Rnds 13-16: Ch 1, sc in last ch-4 sp made, (ch 4, sc in next ch-4 sp) around, ch 1, dc in first sc to form last ch-4 sp.

Rnd 17: Ch 1, sc in last ch-4 sp made, ch 5, (sc in next ch-4 sp, work Picot) twice, ★ sc in next ch-4 sp, ch 5, (sc in next ch-4 sp, work Picot) twice; repeat from ★ around; join with slip st to first sc, finish off: 16 ch-5 sps and 32 Picots.

FIRST SUNFLOWER

Rnd 1 (Right side)**:** With Brown and using smaller size hook, ch 2, 8 sc in second ch from hook; join with slip st to first sc, finish off.

Note: Mark Rnd 1 as **right** side.

Rnd 2: With **right** side facing and using smaller size hook, join Yellow with slip st in any sc; ch 3, (tr, ch 3, slip st) in same st, (slip st, ch 3, tr, ch 3, slip st) in next sc and in each sc around; join with slip st to first slip st, finish off: 8 petals.

Continued on page 17.

Rnd 3: With **right** side facing and using smaller size hook, join Green with sc in any tr; (ch 5, sc in next tr) around, ch 1, tr in first sc to form last ch-5 sp: 8 ch-5 sps.

Rnd 4: Ch 1, (sc, ch 3, sc) in last ch-5 sp made, ★ ch 7, (sc, ch 3, sc) in next ch-5 sp; repeat from ★ around, ch 3; holding Center with **wrong** side facing, slip st in any ch-5 sp on Rnd 17, ch 3; join with slip st to first sc, finish off.

NEXT 14 SUNFLOWERS

Rnds 1-3: Work same as First Sunflower: 8 ch-5 sps.

Rnd 4 (Joining rnd)**:** Ch 1, (sc, ch 3, sc) in last ch-5 sp made, [ch 7, (sc, ch 3, sc) in next ch-5 sp] 5 times, ch 3; holding Center with **wrong** side facing, skip next 2 Picots on Rnd 17 (**before** previous Sunflower) and slip st in next ch-5 sp, ch 3, ★ (sc, ch 3) twice in next ch-5 sp on **new Sunflower**, slip st in corresponding ch-7 sp on **previous Sunflower**, ch 3; repeat from ★ once **more**; join with slip st to first sc on **new Sunflower**, finish off.

LAST SUNFLOWER

Rnds 1-3: Work same as First Sunflower: 8 ch-5 sps.

Rnd 4 (Joining rnd)**:** Ch 1, (sc, ch 3, sc) in last ch-5 sp made, [ch 7, (sc, ch 3, sc) in next ch-5 sp] 3 times, ch 3; holding First Sunflower with **wrong** side facing, slip st in corresponding ch-7 sp, ch 3, (sc, ch 3) twice in next ch-5 sp on **Last Sunflower**, slip st in corresponding ch-7 sp on **First Sunflower**, ch 3, (sc, ch 3) twice in next ch-5 sp on **Last Sunflower**, skip next 2 Picots on Rnd 17 of Center, slip st in last ch-5 sp, ch 3, ★ (sc, ch 3) twice in next ch-5 sp on **Last Sunflower**, slip st in corresponding ch-7 sp on **previous Sunflower**, ch 3; repeat from ★ once **more**; join with slip st to first sc on **Last Sunflower**, finish off.

EDGING

With **right** side facing and using larger size hook, join White with sc in first ch-7 sp on any Sunflower; 6 sc in same sp, ch 3, (skip next ch-3 sp, 7 sc in next ch-7 sp, ch 3) twice, ★ † skip next ch-3 sp, sc in same sp as joining on same Sunflower and in same sp as joining on next Sunflower, ch 3 †, (skip next ch-3 sp, 7 sc in next ch-7 sp, ch 3) 3 times; repeat from ★ 14 times **more**, then repeat from † to † once, skip last ch-3 sp; join with slip st to first sc, finish off.

See Washing and Blocking, page 3.

7. FIELDFLOWERS

Shown on page 10.

Finished Size: $10^{3}/_{4}$" (27.5 cm) diameter

MATERIALS

Bedspread Weight Cotton Thread (size 10):
- White - 77 yards (70.5 meters)
- Green - 13 yards (12 meters)
- Pink - 6 yards (5.5 meters)
- Blue - 6 yards (5.5 meters)
- Yellow - 6 yards (5.5 meters)
- Lavender - 6 yards (5.5 meters)

Steel crochet hook, size 6 (1.80 mm) **or** size needed for gauge

GAUGE SWATCH: $1^{1}/_{2}$" (4 cm) diameter
Work same as Doily through Rnd 3.

STITCH GUIDE

2-DC CLUSTER (uses one st)
★ YO, insert hook in st indicated, YO and pull up a loop, YO and draw through 2 loops on hook; repeat from ★ once **more**, YO and draw through all 3 loops on hook.

3-DC CLUSTER (uses one st or sp)
★ YO, insert hook in st or sp indicated, YO and pull up a loop, YO and draw through 2 loops on hook; repeat from ★ 2 times **more**, YO and draw through all 4 loops on hook.

2-TR CLUSTER (uses next 2 dc)
★ YO twice, insert hook in **next** dc, YO and pull up a loop, (YO and draw through 2 loops on hook) twice; repeat from ★ once **more**, YO and draw through all 3 loops on hook.

DOILY

CENTER

Rnd 1 (Right side)**:** With White, ch 2, 8 sc in second ch from hook; join with slip st to first sc.

Note: Loop a short piece of thread around any stitch to mark Rnd 1 as **right** side.

Rnd 2: Ch 3, dc in same st, 2 dc in next sc and in each sc around; join with slip st to top of beginning ch-3: 16 sts.

Rnd 3: Ch 5 **(counts as first dc plus ch 2, now and throughout)**, (dc in next dc, ch 2) around; join with slip st to first dc: 16 dc and 16 ch-2 sps.